REFLECTIONS FROM LUCERNE –

A COLLECTION

Other Books by Don Davison

An Outline of a Philosophy of the Consciousness of Truth
The Concept of Personhood in the Evolutionary Process of Being
The Game of Life: A Player's Manual for Executives and Others
Sign Posts: A Collection of Essays, Vol. I
Sign Posts: A Collection of Essays, Vol. II
Sign Posts: A Collection of Essays, Vol. III

Poetry

Thoughts and Feelings Book I
Thoughts and Feelings Book II
Needles from the Ponderosas at Zirahuen
Seeds from the Ponderosas at Zirahuen
Pitch from the Ponderosas at Zirahuen
Humus from the Ponderosas at Zirahuen
Sawdust from the Ponderosas at Zirahuen
Sun's rays through the Ponderosas at Zirahuen
Shadows beneath the Ponderosas at Zirahuen
Cones from the Ponderosas at Zirahuen
Pollen sifting from the Ponderosas at Zirahuen
Reflections from Lucerne
Searching Swamps
Questions
Time's Echoes
Memories

Collections

Murmurings
Iris and Other Things
Pieces of the Journey
Through the Swamps of Time
Always Extolling

REFLECTIONS FROM LUCERNE –
A COLLECTION

Don Davison

Zirahuen
Phoenix, AZ
pathtotheself.com
DrDavison@pathtotheself.com

ISBN 978-0-9774039-5-0

Cover and author photos by Patricia Davison.

Special thanks to Louella Holter and Tina Rosio, from W.

To Patricia, for everything.

All of Don Davison's books have water on their covers. Water is one of the most essential attributes of the planet Earth; without it, life as we know it would not exist. It deserves our most considered attention.

Davison's collections of poetry all end with "Finding Pieces." Many of you have asked, where did the rules for the Game of Life come from? They come from many places and different times. Good hunting!

CONTENTS

PEBBLES IN THE SAND

It came to pass –
we touched
and the universe issued forth an ancient note.
Once again when lovers embraced
in the warmth of skin to skin,
reverberations along the X and Y axis
of being's very soul
shuddered in unison.
Murmurings bridged time's immortal gap.
We found each other –
in the streams and lakes,
in the loon's call,
in the moss of swamps,
amongst the pebbles on the shore,
pressed together, silently rocking in ripples,
gently breathing into each other,
kissing lightly as a canoe glides softly
across and through
the surface of God's mirrors.

GOD'S OWN

Old friends pass away,
loneliness sets in,
strength wanes,
dreams die.
And yet …
we must remember:
What good's an old tree?
They stand embattled and somber,
perches for hawks and ravens,
castles for insects,
labyrinths for squirrels,
majestic vectors for new dreams.
So life's gate is closing?
Who cares, we can't stop movement.
The journey was one grand party,
one long stroll through the forest.
Can you recall those times when we came upon an "Oldie,"
an ancient spruce, yellow birch, white pine, oak,
linden, maple, black cherry, tamarack,
Norway pine, butternut, balsam,
aspen, hemlock, ash, cedar
and we stopped awestruck in its presence?

* * *

Know this:
season after season, year after year,
for centuries they lasted beyond their brethren.
Lonesome nights were spent moon-bathed,
listening to the haunting music of owls and coyotes.

They stood forevermore saying only –
"Yes!" to The Father.
What did they know?
What do they know now that we can't grasp?
They know they were born,
lived, and died in His Garden.
And still I wonder, "Where am I?"

SEARCHING

The perceptive "I" sinks into everything,
merging as a confluence,
sending my me into a Taurus
where I meet you and "It."
Our notes are all here and there.
Yet foolishly we insistently hunt for them
and we find them scattered in the cracks
of things, people, and time.
I search for "mine,"
the ever-elusive one,
forever changing as my I
moves towards itself and the other.
In the late evening's winds
and the black-white of pine and snow,
lit by the brilliance of moon and stars,
I listen to Yanni and Bocelli finding theirs,
mine, and everyone's.

SNOW

Jagged intertwined arms of flakes let go of needles
high in the crowns of the ponderosas
crashing, thudding, grating,
reverberating across the cabin roof
with the message of thawing.
Soft comes from someplace,
yet remains hard to purpose,
reminding of moments
when the sharpness of pungent odors
startles one to life
and we take vinegar as refreshment.

STRIFE

How many live close to the line of nothing to eat –
no food, no clothing,
scratching in the dirt among the rocks
in cherty soil
yielding crops of bits of stone?
How many hunting in the desert,
crawling across stones,
kneeling in the sand,
live beseeching The Process?
Who lives searching from dawn to dusk
with bloody hands,
heaving lungs,
and aching heart?
The day finally ends
with a silent explosion
of gold and crimson from north to south
across the western sky.
Hours of agony are washed clean in minutes.
From where does it spring
– the song of the soul?
How is the melody learned?
A subtle aroma comes
and
memories of the sweetness of the wine
say, "L'chayim."

MOONRISE AT SUMMERLAKE

"Dad, I have something to tell you,
I made a mistake."
"Yes, sweetheart. What is it?"
"I've made a decision and I'm not happy."
"Then make another one."

* * *

I was invited to wine, nuts, and her presence,
all delights with which to watch
the rising of the moon.
Just the two of us,
different histories converging in the moonlight.
From the depths of a battered heart
came a history of "The Choice."

* * *

"So … wings on cherubs are small
and flights are short.
You've grown – take flight again.
Remain aloft
until you see more clearly
your own star."
"I'm 30 now and it won't be easy."
"It's true and doesn't matter.
Don't worry and don't wait.
You deserve all the happiness
your heart can hold."
"I need to know I'm right."
"I know,
sometimes it's hard to tell,
when mind and heart are warring."

"I still want what I've always wanted."
"And you should –
your template is an excellent one.
You must move on."
"I know, thank you for listening."
"Thank you for sharing."

* * *

The wine, the peanuts,
the moonrise were wonderful.
And you,
you were the best.

SURVIVORS

There are those who are evolution's gift,
and we also have survived.
At times little have we done to merit accolades.
We are, however, here now.
Is there something we should do?
Yes!
Yes!
And yes again!
Because of the capriciousness of time,
some effort or circumstance,
we are here to present ourselves with our mundane
or sublime involvement,
and yet we spend
or squander precious moments
bought by others in their supreme sacrifice,
by doing so little.

THE CAT

The cat sat idling,
snarling a deep-throated growl.
Then,
purring sounds melted into the stillness
of the overcast day.
A gaping jaw and huge claw
rested gently on the ground.
It was anxious
to pit its strength against the stone,
to scrape and tear sediment from its resting place,
to move and challenge,
mechanical power against the nature of things.

* * *

There was a scratching, scraping, squeaking,
crushing, tearing, jostling
and finally a gentle slope with stumps
where once great trees had stood.
The hill was all broken down,
leveled, torn apart, ravaged.
The cat had won the day.
Claw and jaw marks left in trails
– not for long –
smaller cats would come and smooth
the wounds away.
Neither will the gaping hole in the hillside
remain.
Townhomes will rise in weeks
to grace the horizon,
blocking the view.

THE DEATH OF FIRE

The hot desire to reach out and caress
has long since faded to cold ashes.
You have become like an aging sister
with whom smoldering memories of the past
and anticipations of the future are shared.
Long silences are broken by mundane exchanges.
Although I will see you lovingly through life
all the way to the edge of the grave,
I will not follow you in.
You may ask whose hands have written
the tender tales
of romance and the sharing of passion?
Some by those who've been there,
some by those who will never get there,
and some by those who don't want to go.
To feed, dust and wash clothes is not enough.
Decorating space does not warm the hearth.
Cries and urgings
to keep the flame alive have gone unheeded.
One grows tired,
placing kindling on the fire alone.
I'll stand in deed and need
to help in any way I can
through the coming chapters.
The time has come to walk alone
on starry nights and in drenching rain.
Mist and mystery beckons.
Adieu. Adios. Good-bye.
May all that is good
be by your side forever.
Love.

THE FAMILY

A holy sanctuary,
the beginning of ourselves
from ties that bind us to who and what we are
– almost –
to flowing matter
free to choose
to mix and love.
Slowly,
enough of everything
gives each of us to ourselves.
Fast enough to respond to the winds of flux.
We must live by respecting primeval laws,
bending,
blending,
becoming one,
learning to love the All.
Death leaves opportunities,
annual rings,
new growth,
a strength of seasons,
a dedication to purpose,
a family shrine.
L'chayim!
Abba!

THE FLAME

Years melt
as orange-black tongues
lick away your layered life
leaving white-gray, hoary, wavering remnants
bellowing in the conflagration.
To what great purpose must we
put our pens to paper
in your soft warmth and light?
Is it only to add our whimperings to the chorus
of our fellows
or is it to sing your praise forever?

THE RANCH

A piece of ground
laden with early family memories
and the transformation of raw llano
to fields of grain,
orchards, and rows of vegetables.
Adobe blocks and rocks rose into walls
forming houses, surrounded by trees.
The inside filled with a courtyard, a pool,
tables and chairs, and bodies
bathed with water, sun, and love.
Children playing, the gamut of pets,
watchful caretakers,
family discussions, celebrations,
visits of friends, relatives, and fellow scientists,
all were welcome.
And always the lingering smell
of damp, musty, cold stone
melting into heat sinks
when fires shedding flickering light
emanated a special warmth among presences,
family members each and every one.
A place and a litany of shared moments,
35 years of them and still counting,
waxing and waning in their singularity,
shedding and donning the coats of youth and death,
behind doors of ecstasy and pain.

THE REUNION

The reunion was at hand.
They gathered from distant places
from divergent paths of life.
All separated
by time and space
experienced alone in search of self.
Finally,
in the presence of each other,
in the webbing of the mitochondria,
shines the same light from twinkling eyes.
Long gazes and deep laughter
sent messages of love tumbling over each other
as the warmth of a family
enveloped four generations.
It was a special time and place
where many became one,
and fertilized from afar,
still gave birth to others of their kind.

SHOVEL

Where there were willing hands and back
you took your turn
with bits and pieces of the orb.
To shrink from the mounds and depths
you were unable.
Faithful to your purpose,
you made mountains accessible
and valleys bloom.
Now you lean against the far wall of the shed,
handle worn, heel and toe bearing marks
of man's intrusive insistence.
Time and time again
in the face of the interminable,
you did your tasks.
From you and the history of your efforts
much have I learned,
leaning upon you more than once
during brief thoughtful respites
on the way to the eternal.

THE STRANGER

We stare at the far horizon,
eyes fixed beyond the now.
Stumbling through lost and perfidious ways,
then, smitten by a movement,
curiosity overwhelms.
A limping man interdicts our way.
The stranger's presence beckons.
The mind shouts,
"Who? Where? How? Why?"
The contingencies of supposed
and philosophic truths,
idealism – realism
and all the other newer relative -isms
clash and fall into the unknown.
Is there any truth beyond which we cannot go,
one founding mental space where truth
forever stays the same?
Yes!
In Him, through Him and by Him
I draw the picture of myself.
Now and forever He will be my brother.

THE WALKER

Assessing and compounding
my current circumstance
leads to scattered thoughts and tattered nerves.
The complexity of modern life
bemoaned to the nth degree,
the IRS and taxes, debts, bills, generators, snowplows,
a personal dilemma,
grandchildren, a business and cash flow.
On drifting mental currents comes a phrase:
"Kierkegaard's simple man."
Where are you?
I rambled on floating back and forth
across the edges of my ignorance –
then I saw him walking straight and proud
heading north towards the reservation
– alone.
In the midst of a driving snowstorm,
the northern half of the state
under a winter storm watch.
With all eyes glued to forecasts and announcements –
he walked into the wind-driven flakes
oblivious to my difficulties
and the world's concerns.
How could he know mine or I his?

TOO FAST

We read from left to right at some frenetic pace
– those of us who still read –
at a pace that starts in the present
and moves into an unknown future.
Others read from right to left,
away from the confusion of the now.
Is theirs a path to the wisdom of yesterday?
We need those fixed points
to help us frame the Right
for the now and possibly for tomorrow.

THE LONG HAUL
OR THE SHORT SHIFT

Is there a difference in the warriors?

* * *

The one who with one swift blow
sends a despot to his grave
or a dragon to its death?
Who saves the maiden, town, or kingdom
with one mighty
move of his swift sword?
One second or one bold afternoon
in which history meets a crossroad and is written.
A courageous momentary commitment
and in fame and victory basks the hero.

* * *

The battle not yet here – the cause not quite clear,
at the ready now and tomorrow
– and tomorrow never comes.
Sunny days, the clouds, wind, fatigue,
and time draws on.
The enemy within draws down the sword
to dull the edge.
Sleep calls and days turn into years.
The battle is never fought.
Yet the steel of commitment
keeps ready the blade.

* * *

The deed that is done and won
or the one who is always ready –
both win!

The laurel to the hourglass whose sands
forever flow,
and to those who maintain a course of joy
to live at the edge of the canyon;
one to leap into battle when the time is right,
and the other to guard against the need to fight.
Both know the deed.
It is to be real in the now!

WHAT'S REAL?

Thoughts swirl in pools.
Words whirl,
mixing with what I knew
or thought I knew.
Then it all melts into the indistinct:
Mine? Not Mine?
Who can tell?
Leaning on the cuff of those who've gone before,
I question,
"Am I becoming what William said we all were
– full of sound and fury, signifying nothing?"

WINTER WALK

White, snow-striped, black ponderosa trunks,
shrouded with frozen gifts,
holding more in their shaggy manes,
stood as sentinels sharing soft wind notes.
My face is touched by bellowings
out of the northeast.
A bathing winter moon
casts a shifting pale on the landscape,
as sweet pungent smoke
drifts into my eyes and nostrils.
My chilled body,
caught in a sub-zero embrace,
listens to squeaking crystals
crunching beneath footfalls.

TUMBLEWEEDS

In the early fall
– you are my Gethsemane.
Your flowers hint of purple passion
leading to thorns.
I gently grasp your stalks,
yet I feel the prick.
In tearing out your roots
my soul is cleansed
as I seek to eliminate your presence
from my life.
The seasons flow into years
and I find:
In pain there is life.
In life there is hope.
In hope there is death.
In your crown of thorns there is Eternal Life.

YES? NO? I DO NOT KNOW!

How much time do I have?
There is only the now in which to say,
"I love you."
And to whom is this addressed?
To the All and therefore
as a gift of It to me.
To myself, that mantle of personhood
that eternally shrouds my all,
to her, and to all of them.
And in that I say,
"Mea culpa,
Mea culpa,
Mea maxima culpa."
Forgive me
for what I have done
and for what
I have failed to do.
The Origin of Being houses everything.
The feminine gives birth.
The world/multiverse gives a place.
And You, You give hand and heart
into which I pour my being.
You are forever for whom,
through whom,
by whom
my life takes shape.
The trails of these encounters reek
with the sweat of decisions
of a being on purpose with
self and circumstance.
What is one?
How much of the other?

Again,
and again:
How much is too much?
How much is too little?
Yes?
No?
I do not know!
Yet I continue to come from the Origin of Being,
to contact with the feminine and others.
As I drip my blood into life's crucible,
I say only, "Amen."

YOUR PRESENCE

Like sun-baked gold the ponderosa's pollen
shares Your presence.
The flickerings of Your heart's candle
flash amidst the distant rumblings of autumn rain.
Sights and sounds of infinite shadows
light Your path,
echoing among the mountains
like honey and amber.
They bring me to You,
clinging to the remnants of Your cloak.
I pull the coverlet from my ears and eyes
that I may better see Your celebration
in the late night sky.
The notes merge,
becoming one sound with the footsteps
of Your rain.
I am reminded,
Your path is lit, the music playing,
Your voice saying,
"Come dance with me!"

AGING

If the movement of our lives is the sole reason
that we harbor a penchant for entropy,
we lie.
Can't we remember that the children of yesterday,
awe-struck with curiosity,
jumped in puddles and chased butterflies?
And don't we know that the children of forever
always come
crossing the threshold of wonder?
Now I leave the stage
to let come that second act.
Hope is one of the eternal triad's stepping stones,
and you, death cannot follow.
I linger not in passing,
I am already dancing
in the twinkling eyes of the young.

AGONY

How could it be that love's song
is sung now in such hurtful notes
when ecstasy was her only gift?
He had asked only to be touched
and an angel came.
Now,
it was as if a fire burned around an empty shell.
No feelings took harbor
in his twisted, tortured soul.
Breathing in shallow rasping gasps,
his aching heart had no desire
to pump life-blood through
a hollow core.
He screamed,
"Have I lived in the shadow of the wolf
long enough?
How long must I stand beside my dead mate?"
Wracked with sobbing he whispered,
"When can I cut the bonds and be free?"
Creeping into the crypt beneath the chapel
(how close could a sinful knight
get to the sanctuary?)
and lying naked on the cold stone floor,
he begged for forgiveness.
Moaning, he cried out,
"What happens to a frozen soul?"
Haunting images of passion's fire
dripping perspiration
into warm fingers in the throes of touching moments flitted
through his mind.

Now,
tongues of ice seemed to come from the stone
to lick his clammy skin.
Would this searing agony ever leave
his wounded heart?
Could he ever stand bathed in the sun's warmth
or the moon's glow and be whole
in body and in spirit?
Kneeling, he sobbed,
"One needs only to love to be loved.
And when it comes, how are we to own it?
Are the Savior's arms our only repose?"
From the silent sepulcher the angel's voice spoke,
"Now!
Now you are free to touch and be touched.
Now you can open your arms to a sacramental union.
Now you may feel again the ecstasy of love."

ARRESTED

Brilliant rays
slip from beneath the clouds,
chasing crystals of life's liquid
into rivulets
that in leaving branches
crash against the rocks,
bathing moss in mist,
while a spectrum hangs gently
in the light.

BROKEN MIRROR

In the season of repose,
while feeling lost and searching
for the beneficence of spirit,
I behold a broken mirror.
Life's eternal silver shadows
lay like fading slivers
in musty savorings of fantasy and history.
Scattered shards of shattered times,
tears and untold tales, laughter and reflection,
lay consigned to tombs.
The silver has left the mirror –
frayed images hover only at edges.
Receding memories of pondered passion
lay curled and dying in the corners of an empty frame.
Dream's circle,
severed by gales of perturbing absences,
issues no rhapsody.
Finally,
from a core of aching exhaustion,
loneliness breaks out.
Questions of being seep to the surface:
Who am I?
What have I become that
dying dreams haunt my holy time?
Where are scenes imagined, felt, hoped for,
visions clearly seen with the mind's eye,
deeply etched in the soul's heart?
Too long and too little
I have been stroked by cold hands
devoid of practiced touch.

Where must I go? To whom can I turn?
I run and run and run,
seeking in my pain some semblance of the serene.
Then,
in scaling a mountain I am led to a lake,
where in the exuberance and grandeur of God's flush,
I find in the surface of still water
a mirror unbroken.

DAMN QUESTIONS!

Is it the buck that chases with lust in his heart,
or the doe that leads to warm her womb?
Does it matter?

DEAD DREAMS

Although we may eschew their pounding rhythm
and late night presence,
along with dried curled leaves nestled in eddies
and brown fronds of pine lying in flat arrays,
they are tinder for passion's spark.
I didn't sit long enough beneath the crowns,
running fingers through lacy soft leaves
or smooth new needles.
I didn't remain in the seasons
next to ponderosa trunks,
hands stroking crevices in the bark.
Confirms the adage:
Hope's eternal
when my I pushes towards an Infinite One,
seeking self.

EARTH DAY '98

We crush the backs of mountains
and from their powder mixed with water
make a slurry.
Then pouring it into vertical and horizontal forms,
we create roads, floors, walls, and ceilings.
Covering the scarred earth with gray slabs
on which we walk, eat, make love, hang pictures,
sleep, drive and play.
All this wouldn't be so bad but today,
even though I braked my car,
the squirrel got confused
and turned back towards the safety of the road
and died.
The blip, blip of my tires telegraphed the deadly notes.
My body shuddered and my inner voice screamed, "No! No!"
Again the question comes:
Must our presence always leave
a destructive track upon the earth?

FANTASY

Fantasy as ideal moments
come when unknown antecedents
give birth
in the mirror of self.
There are smells, sights, sounds, tastes,
and touch,
touch eternally
the exclamation point.
Subtleties unfold in the wilderness of the universe,
rising up, overwhelming us with
Yes! Yes!
And yes again!
The question:
How do those soul-stirring evocative waves of images
and feelings surge to the forefront
of our intellectual, emotional, physical,
and spiritual loci?
Who knows?
And yet pressing themselves into all four theaters
of our personhood,
soul nectar drips through a vortex
into passion's fire and flares,
consummating our being.
Still we ask …
What are those ingredients
that fire the themes and images
of fantasy?
From where do they come,
those clear elements that congeal
in such sacred soul pictures?

Do massaging fingers
set stages for turbulent syntheses'
melting exposures that tease curiosity
fed by wonder's golden gate?
Are we too early swung to the windward,
caught in a holy gale that salts the glaze of our goblets
with reflections of mystery,
compelling us to seek in forever wanderings?
Driven by loins and hearts of uncertain integrity
we follow the muse of self from cauldron to cauldron,
knowing someplace in the depths of one,
Always! Never! Always! Never! Always! Never!

HEROIC ANGEL

You came with the rising of October's fullness,
dancing on The Peaks
and leaping with your rich golden vestments
into the darkness of the night.
I was standing in the shadows
at the edge of the meadow,
lost in my desert of project-oriented masculinity
and frustrated in my connection to my self.
Errant arms encircled dead dreams,
circumscribing empty space,
holding nothing.
Dropping to my side
you touched me and spoke with a voice of amber.
You called me
and I reached out with purposeful hands;
in touching you they touched the land,
they went everyplace.
Listening to your beautiful voice,
I learned so much about sharing the munificence
of each passing moment.
You held me resting in your arms.
I was resurrected.
New life shot through the axis of my being,
nostrils were filled with an aroma
so sweet, so soft, as if the essence of the earth
became unto frankincense and myrrh.
Skylights became forever clear windows
to heaven's manifold graces.
I looked into the green eyes of nature's spirit and said, "Yes!"
I poured my being into you
in thought, word, and deed.
A wolf basked in the sun
and bathed in the juices of fecund.

"Know the beauty and freedom of your soul"
was the message you shared with me,
and I learned to love again.
We shared new truths:
Icons of ages past do not fit a kingdom that is at hand.
Struggling with ourselves,
we accept the gauntlet of the present.
You spoke to me of marriage and of vows.
All I could say was,
"Yes, I will meet you in the holy of holies,
where together we will dedicate our wills to a mission of loving
self and others."
You took me to His House to meet Him.
Awestruck, I stood frozen,
caught in the darkness by the roots of my ineptitudes.
In searching His face,
I lingered at the edges of His laughing eyes
and busied myself collecting tears.
A small crystal goblet,
carved by the keeper of hope and presented to me,
was used to catch His gifts of mirth.
You said these tears were to be used as nectar
for soul-saving nourishment,
when I was lost and wandering in deserts of pain,
seeking soft solutions to life's onslaught of choices.
This semi-salty liquid would send
honest messages of bittersweet ingredients
into life's great banquet of truths, enabling me,
as I sought to know,
to accept less control
and be content with the truth of the now.
You forced me to build a house of faith
and master the mantra,
"I live now, not I, but You live within me."

You said,
"Let these tears sustain a catharsis
as your 'I' emerges from your 'me'
and becomes one with the All."
Suspended in the aroma of balsams,
lost in the gentle breeze of the moon's wake,
swept up by your holy innocent presence,
I wept.
Two slept together as the Word became flesh.
Cherubs chanted while harps and flutes
were played by celestial minstrels.
Murmurings folded into,
"To have and to hold until death do you part."
I awoke and turned to thank you and you were gone.
Just the hem of your heavenly cloak was visible
as you sped away into the stars.
Your divine presence slipped into the ephemeral,
leaving me to a life of flesh and bone,
ecstasy and sorrow.
And I,
I chose the angel's remnants
standing beside me in the shadows.
I shouted after your spirit,
"Yes! Yes! And yes again!"
Then I heard you whisper,
"As it was in the beginning,
it is now,
and forever shall be."

HIS TRACKS

And it came to pass –
from cacophonous rumblings of heaven's bowels
and hiccups of brilliant flashes,
through a gray unknown formlessness,
a nectar spilled upon the earth
in tat-ta-tat rhythm,
the passing cadence of the walking God,
leaving silver mirrors caught in droplets
slipping to the ends of pine needles,
and for a single instant
holding in a tiny, crystal, teardrop track
the essence of all life.
A white not white,
a gray not gray,
a silver not silver,
a shimmering, transparent, flowing journey
of soft truth enveloping touches
bathing senses
and finally dropping
to congeal in scattered pools
reflecting God's every yes!

I AM

I am windswept in the mind,
tossed far beyond my shore.
Where am I?
And worse,
Who am I?
Where is my Lucerne?
I could not stand with St. Bernard –
covering my eyes at the beauty of the lakes.
My soul seeks the reflections of His gifts,
the teardrops of His soul
as they splash upon the rocks along His shores.

LULLABY FOR GRANDCHILDREN

Squashed like a blue bug.
Chased by a butterfly.
Niki, Niki, Nu,
Where are you?
Big fat dinosaur
swimming on the moon.
Niki, Niki, Nu,
How are you?
Little bitty bird
picking up an elephant.
Niki, Niki, Nu,
I know you.
Flying piece of yellow cheese
hanging on a cloud.
Niki, Niki, Nu,
I love you.

NOISE

What wisdom washes from the gargling of the ravens
as they greet the new day?
Is it an awe-inspiring prayer of thanksgiving,
or just banter on the lack of carrion?

ONE MORE – ONE LESS

You came running low, legs stretching,
streaking across the meadow,
ears flat, nose pointed, eyes fixed.
And I,
caught in my spring reverie,
thought you ran from the grating sounds of my sled
as I brought tanks to my cabin.
I'd been lost in the nuptials of blue birds and ravens,
smelling deep the freshness of thawing,
and then I saw you.
At full tilt you reached down with snapping jaws
and caught a prairie dog playing in the snow.
Crunching it between your teeth you came to a stop.
Glancing my way
you seemed to say,
"And you?"
As you spun and trotted away,
I hope you heard my cry.
I shouted,
"Yeah!
Get 'em!
Wild puppy,
Get 'em!"

ORCHARD FOUND

Returning from the hunt,
high in the hills,
I caught a faint hint of blossoms.
With heaving lungs yet hot from the kill,
I rushed headlong
into a garden of perfume.
Of a sudden there was a handmaiden lying
in His orchard.
All is but a bit of Eden next to Paradise.
Locks of golden straw hid fruit.
A dark forest sheltered a cavern.
Green sparkling eyes beckoned,
laden with pink and white petals.
I reached high to touch pistil and stamen
while drinking from the tips of fountains.
In time I came to know the whole orchard.
There were rolling hills and deep gullies
all scenting of you mixed with linen and wool.
A ferret's secret den was opened.
Dancing touches secured treasure from its stores.
Whimpering you came.
And I,
thrusting my wolf's head
into the dampness of the antechamber of your womb,
found paradise.

PREFACE

The shining of cupid's arrow
adds madness to the luster of our dreams.
And while we are caught in streams of desert sands
scorching the bottoms of our feet,
we dance
in the gleam of Lucifer's eyes.
Probingly he says,
"Hawker of wares, what sell you but words?"
"Melodies of soul," I say.

PRIMAL SCREAM

How large the party?
God's diamond is huge, its facets many.
The primal scream's more than a wailing sound
or a whining voice.
It's a celebration of life, of everything.

SIMPLE SOUL

I am a woodcutter, a simple man.
Not a nobleman, someone with high history.
Sometimes I think it would be nice to be a stonecutter,
creating beautiful blocks that will stand against time,
sheltering holy gatherings.
And then ...
I reflect –
If it were not for warm hearths
and good food,
I doubt those voices I hear in prayer
and raised in song
would have such vigor
nor harbor so much joy.
Simple things
that feed the body
and our souls
are the real building blocks of life.

THE STAGE

I peer out from behind the ponderosas
and step to the edge of a meadow amphitheater.
With trepidation, I enter.
What role will I play?
My entrance made,
the theme envelops me.
His promptings pull me towards a purpose.
Divine Goodness always takes center stage.
Walking confidently to a place right of center
and raising my arms and voice,
I fall to my knees and simply say,
"Yes!"

SLOWING

The gift of age
is learning to pace one's self.
Or, is it that I cross the bridge of the millennium
at 50-plus
with stirrings of conflicting purpose
mixed with fading hope?
Is age that essential spice,
stimulating taste buds
into rhythmic ruminatory mastication,
giving life a gentle spark?

TGIF

The hustle, bustle and rustle of numbers
inundates my taxed sensitivities
and thrusts a backdrop of dissonance
into my workplace.
Suddenly,
a calm settles and serenity reigns.
Briefly I wallow in a respite from tempest's times.
Awestruck,
I behold empty walkways and vacant benches.
Everyone's gone someplace else.
Strolling down deserted pathways,
space saturates my soul.
Finally,
I sense that elusive peace.
My fatigued body is showered with a quiet fullness,
bathing in a well-being so essential
to the depth of repose.
Is there anything better than a campus
on a beautiful Friday afternoon?

THE APOGEE

And so ...
We came to the edges of savannas,
then to extended horizons.
Walked and sailed to every continent,
saw every shore,
scaled every peak.
As we cast information into space,
following with ourselves,
unlimited possibilities emerged.
Capturing the electron
let us power numerous gadgets
and dream of harboring vast amounts of data.
Now,
virtual vistas,
filled with rampant movement and background noise,
abound.
Yet I do not eat in gigabytes,
nor do I think in nanoseconds.
Human time's my fare.
What makes me feel whole
are sights, sounds and smells
of traversed tracts of the orb.
And, oh yes!
Those tastes that shake memory's fuzz
and titillate a million dreams.
They say we'll visit other galaxies,
that we'll find other planet homes.
The stars are where it's at!
I speculate and say,
"Perhaps."
And then I add,
"Not this one!"

At 56,
and on the threshold of the 21st century,
I won't be making any long trips.
Sure …
I could have a clone way out there someplace.
What difference would it make?
Being belongs to itself and "I" wouldn't be there.
I wouldn't want to be.
I'm too busy reveling
in the depths of my current existential soup.

THE AWARD

The Ministerial Group agreed:
Never to ourselves!
We serve a different meal,
one of mutual support.
Our lives share a message from the depths
of chosen professions:
The rewards of simply knowing we serve
the Truth of One,
sustaining vocations wrought in the crucible
of Divine guidance and commitment.
This award will be for
"Other chosen ones"
who labor in His vineyard,
many times alone.
Reaching out we will touch them
with the coming of a drop of nectar
for their chalice or goblet,
the sweet taste of a "Thank you!"
and "Well done!"
will serve as saint's fare
in a world's desert of separation.
Yet we must be careful
not to reward too often the clay feet
of wandering beleaguered souls,
knowing that some turn to benevolence
in troubled times,
and when blessings mount
forget the testing times of seasons yet to come.

WHERE?

Are there always Dragon Winds?
Must cyclones of duty threaten one's days and nights?
Do those hot and cold places of focused energy
in time bind souls to agonized deaths?
May I find a grotto warm and moist,
with a gentle pulling
that releases a cascade of flowing creativity
merging with quiescence.
The sacred and mundane,
we always say the sacred first
– and yet –
trifle endlessly with the mundane.
Where is your castle, My Lord?
Where is your fortress where none may insist
and repose is always at hand?
Is it in saying yes to all in need?

WISCONSIN SPRING

The white has slipped away.
Gray-brown reigns with evergreen punctuations.
Geese call from formations backdropped by silver clouds
sprinkled with ashes.
Softly, silently, gently
You lay your fingers upon the land.
Pale shades of everything shimmer
in breeze-touched caresses.
Spring comes!
Monet's pastels hint again
and render ephemeral suggestions.
Shoots slip from fertile tombs.
Hope splashes across God's canvas.
Crocus and daffodils launch their colors.
Fragrance of mold's lusty purpose
permeates waiting nostrils.
Eyes, hungry for color,
scan south sides and eddies.
Whistles and warblings wander though morning's mist.
Languages of season's change mix.
Sleeping life stretches and smiles at itself.
Dandelions' maned golden heads roar.
Blades of broken tan share space with green slivers.
Winged creatures whisk about.
Buds break scaled and sealed treasures.
Veined felt fingers unfold.
Delicate lace shrouds the crowns of trees.
Willows speak in fuzzy tongues.
Cattails bob swollen heavy heads losing hair.
Turtles bask in fleeting rays.
Trilliums hang smiling at the forest floor.
Bloodroots share white brilliance.

Spring beauties and Dutchman's breeches
dance in droves.
Searching loon lyrics send echoes
bouncing off gray mirrors.
The aurora borealis bathes night skies.
Owls insist.
Maple leaves droop in miniature canopies.
The oak dangles stubby fingers.
Most just uncurl and unfurl.
Blueberry bushes sport tiny dots of possibilities.
Naked branches where once hung life say,
"It's done!"
Cherry blossoms shout.
From the prairies of the Southwest
to the woods of the North,
all across the land
spring comes!

* * *

And I, I just stand panting.
Awe has drained me of my strength and senses.
Spring comes and comes and comes!

DECISIONS

In the constellation of my moment
all my river-paths have broken ice –
save one.
I'm battered with a vision
of necessity, duty, honor, and history.
It shrouds me, penetrating all my soul-waking hours.
To begin again,
in the midst of life,
is not an easy thing.
To produce clarity of soul,
bespeaking a holy purpose,
is always the greatest challenge.
One cannot abandon another –
nor is that the objective.
The gift of freedom is the only choice.
To stand and do with passion is the thing!
And what about those haunting dreams –
and time?
They must be lived with equanimity,
as souls bend magnanimously,
birthing tranquility.
And yet, and still,
there are always "others" in our space.
So?
Freedom is theirs and choice is always made
in the context of the now.
The fire will always and forever be:
"True! Mine! Now!"

One must add to the embers
and we can only add
the Truth of One.
Still, lingering thought remains,
whose responsibility to hold the mirror?
Always, always one's own,
mine for me
– and mine for them.

HIGH TENSION POLE

Naked vestige,
where were you born
and what fertile circumstance
brought you to your stature?
Your cellulose heart,
preserved in creosote or penetrol,
locks you to your current sentence.
Linked to dead brothers and sisters,
the grandeur of your courage
brought you through the vagaries of the seasons.
You did not break then,
nor does your current task deter you from
gracing skylines.
You are tall,
taller than all the surrounding trees,
and slender, elegant simplicity,
purposeful in your stark presence.
Holding giga-volts,
you are resigned in death
to line highways and byways.
As we rush in our communal disrespect,
may the softness of dawns and dusks manifest
your untiring commitment to stand
as a reminder of your former self.
Lush spruce,
bedecked with boughs laden with needles of essence,
stately tree of slopes,
know that we remember
how you held the chickadee and squirrel,
raven and marten,
and caught moonlight in dark drooping arms,
sending haunting shadows
flitting across snow.

MEMORY

Time –
A changing scene,
now closer, now farther away,
the fading taste of a lover's lips,
trails of perfume hinting presence,
a sound.
All becoming echoes
in the recesses
of the mind.

POINT OF VIEW

The wind said to the rock,
"Why are you so still?"
The rock answered the wind,
"Because I can't move."
Then the wind sighed to the rock,
"I will swirl about and caress you."
The rock responded to the wind,
"Then we both will be in the arms of the Cosmic God."

SECRET PLACES

My trail to the present
was through the forest,
that dense space graced with shadowed presences
and dark forms giving birth to sun-lit dreams.
I come to you from fallen timber,
trunks and branches ready for resurrection
or new-found graves.
Some for posts, others lintels,
and still others
stoops, sills, rafters, hidden places and walls.
Each and every one, food for passion's plate.
Others will rest at our bedside
or in vaulted space created for shelter and wonder.
And not a few will warm the hearth
and light the soul's path.
They say I am not of this age.
Perhaps they are right.
I was cast into the swamps of time
listening always to echoes in the silence.
Echoes becoming omnipresent symphonies
creating for me castles, serf's huts,
and always those Nordic cabins for love and life.
They say we will live twice as long as we used to.
It wouldn't matter.
The basket of dreams will last forever.

SUPPLICATION

I want to lie with you
in the dampness of spring.
Play with you
in the softness of summer.
Sleep with you
in the crispness of fall.
Weep with you
in the chill of winter.
I want to spend my waking moments
nuzzling gentle exchanges
into conversations that spring
from souls' centers.
Oh, silent swamp!
Oh, gentle spruce!
How long, how long must I lie beyond touch,
lost in chaos?

SWALLOWS IN THE WIND

What abundance of hope springs from nature's face!
The efforts of small,winged creatures
defy comprehension.
How are we to read Nature's exclamation points?
Just as they are!
And so …
at the end of the day,
battered and weary,
I picture a soft morning sky
with swallows in the wind.

TEARS

The cavern is weeping,
tears of joy are falling.
The wolf is howling,
full of desire.
The leaves of the quaking aspen
shimmer in the moonlight.
The owl sweeps the soft new snow
of the arctic night.
We came hungry to the shores of our youth,
then,
we dined at a great banquet.
The repast gave birth to other courses
of our own flesh.
All becoming the pride
of our hearts.
You are moss, you are water,
you are willow soft and subtle.
Now quickly does the fox
take the partridge from the knoll.
Liquid gold pours from our reverie
and we bathe in each other's sweat.

DISTURBING THE PEACE

Where, oh where, is peace?
Communities of the new century
meet in mega-malls before and after
– the movies.
Is there some erosion,
degradation of human life,
when bombastic noise envelopes
every body in every space?
We sit in jets for hours
listening to headphones
and the roaring onslaught of engines.
Who speaks of Jet Lag,
disorientation,
assaulted senses?
Vibrations shatter
the diligent rhythms
of organisms' gentle play.
How much more of the fragmentation
of evolution's gifts of pace, peace,
and silence must we lose?

THE TRYST

I ran to the swamp
in orgasmic pursuit.
You were
among the balsam and white pine
lying in wait.
Circling in the sphagnum moss,
princess pine, and wintergreen,
I watched you sleep.
Your breasts gently rising,
your hair wafting in the soft breeze.
A branch broken
by a buck or doe
startled you.
Seeing me you smiled
and jumped up running
through the cedars toward the creek.
I caught you at the water's edge in the damp saw grass
and laid you on a hillock.
We came together as an osprey screeched for its mate,
and leaving us to quiescence
in the swamp's silent cradle,
she flitted along still water
through sunlight and shadow,
sending trout darting.

TIME'S SADDLE

They come sitting time's saddle,
left stirrup the past,
right the future,
always leaning towards one or the other.
Forever
following the trail of in-between.
Never and always,
now and then,
I ride and ride the present.

SEEKING A YES!

And ...
the questions persist.
Where is that Og Mandino moment,
that one sale –
my daughter to herself,
my sons to theirselves,
my grandchildren to themselves,
my wife to herself,
me to myself?
The breeze is light.
The scent of moisture hangs
on the fingers of the breeze.
The temperature is just right.
The view of the meadow is pleasing eyes.
Its midsummer attire a full wardrobe
of dazzling delight.
Shocked from my mind's camera,
my eyes focus on the multicolored garden of people,
all busy eating in the mall's food court
with every palate enjoying a simple yes!
and conversation bubbling from every table.
Why is this so hard?

CACTUS ROSE

When running through the high desert
and reflecting on the encroaching human effect
of agriculture,
I pined for the desert's wilderness
of "yesterday" and "before."
Then …
God's omnipresent effervescence
presented in the moistness of a vale
the lingering essence of a cactus rose.

EMPORIUMS OF E-COMMERCE

Pathros would be proud.
He'd see the emporiums of the day
amassing goods from every continent and island.
From Pakistan and New Zealand,
Canada and Costa Rica, Brazil and Denmark,
Hong Kong and Iceland, China and the United States,
Borneo and Bolivia.
Great caravans of sky birds, streams of flotillas,
roaring wagons, some with two trailers,
as well as trudging fire barrels
followed by long lines of serpentine boxes,
come laden with cargo
for Home Depots, Sam's Clubs, Bath and Beyonds,
Cashways, megastores for mega-malls.
Where does hand touch hand and eye meet eye?
Only at the checkout counter does someone
scan your wares and look up to say
with extended hand
"That will be $137.48 please,
and have a nice day!"
And so ...
we enter the third millennium.
Our friend plied his trade before the first.
Would he wonder whose hand extends
robes to cover the poor?
Would he ask,
What is the interchange?

And where is that brother to sister union
when someone gets something from someone
they really need now?
E-Commerce they call it.
From what source the loving interchange that says,
"Here, take this, you need it"?

WIND

We hide from wind scourgings
– except in spring –
blanketed,
we wait, scenting moisture's presence.

TOUCHINGS

I have squeezed myself
from antechamber to foyer in less than a century.
Meanwhile,
I delighted in sharing
the touchings of my being.
For to whom do we owe our presence,
but to it all?

MERCADO DE ABASTOS

I'm strolling on a brilliant summer day
through a Mexican market.
What more does anyone want?
Smells of the richness of the earth's fertility
spill into walkways and linger,
bundled in corners.
I notice a tree,
that for decades
struggled to share its presence
with bent shoulders of vendors
as they clean fruit and vegetables,
hawking wares of every description,
inviting consumers to partake.
The roof of a shoe stall cuts off its life.
No one notices.
From my elitist rage,
my eyes fix on the garbage
strewn from top to bottom.
Questioning a culture's lassitude
and lack of understanding,
touting the conservationist's position of the day,
the deeper (deepest) ecology
and Nature's marvelously efficient abundance,
I malign the waste in the marketplace.
Then, suddenly,
I turn the corner into the flower market
and bathed in awe and shame,
stand still
as I, and ants, and butterflies
take sustenance from it all.

NEW WARRIORS

We have left La La Land.
We have now entered
the Real World of the Now.
Where are the warriors of the moment?
The man or woman who says,
"Touch me,
or anyone in my presence inappropriately
with malicious intent,
and I will administer
what I perceive to be sufficient force
– up to and including lethal –
to protect myself and others."
No one has the right to harm the innocent.
On my watch,
I will not let it pass.

NOTE TO THE PERSECUTED

For those who have been persecuted
over the centuries
and for those who are newcomers
to this bestial arena,
we know that you will understand:
The Truth of the Now
does not mean that we will forget,
ever!
It means we will live
with justice in our hearts, minds, and actions
because we know now.
And precisely because we remember,
we will put *every* member of the species
in the human circle.
All the while laboring with every ounce of effort
to give to each an opportunity to glow
with creative genius,
using their energies for the pursuit of
life, liberty, and happiness.

RETURNING

I've been to Bangkok and London,
to Montevideo and Rome.
I've been to Mexico City,
to Victoria.
I've been to Los Angeles
and New York.
I've been to Nairobi,
to Cape Town.
Why is it then that when I think of returning
it is always to Otter Creek?
I must return again and again
to Otter Creek.

OUR PURPOSE

What a species!
We build with anxious hearts
revetments for cannon and searchlights.
And a hundred years later they entertain pets
and our children.

PEOPLE

Whether movement at the edges
or in the heart of the whole,
does it matter where we are?
New countries with lots of space,
old countries with lots of people,
Where is the balance?
Certainly not with any kind of nationalism;
we all belong to the world.
We must own this universal truth.
Yet we wonder,
"Are there enough secluded valleys
for each member of the species
to have their chateau?"
No, not hardly,
and there will always be those
who would not want that kind of life.
Truth is that freedom of choice that defines human life.
Fraternité!
Liberté!

SEEKING

We crave sensing the effort of the human soul.
And so …
pause next to a trestle, see, feel, and hear
the iron horse galloping, its iron hooves clanging
on iron rails stretching across continents.
Stand in the concrete canyons of the great cities.
Be gathered in by the bustle and hustle of those
wandering the streets.
Feel the presence of those hiding behind
closed doors and windows.
Enter a centuries-old cathedral.
Watch children play and laugh.
Hold the hands of the elderly and hope.
Let awe sink into your bones and wonder.
Live seeking, always seeking!

REMEMBER

Artisans' bent backs and nimble hands
give birth to myriad forms.
When,
from these multifarious creations
of mind and soul
bedecking the markets of the world,
you select a friend's gift,
remember in giving that one piece,
God smiles.

SNATCHES

Fields of headstones and crowds of faces,
symbols of minds' aspirations.
Desires and dreams,
do they matter if we don't remember them?
Yes and no.
Yes, because of justice,
no, because of justice.
Yet ...
we must always remember two hands
are stronger than one.
We are always from another.
There was forevermore,
more than one.

I DO! I DO!

In my monkish mullings
I find myself wishing,
"I need to live in a stone house!"
Then,
as I glance into a glassed picture,
I see a reflection of my stone walls
and as the lamplight illuminates
umber and charcoal,
I say,
"I do! I do!"

IS THIS REALLY NEWS?

Tristan and Isolde tell us:
The artful presentation of news
is a challenge for the minds and media
of the day.
"Gigo" and more "Gigo"
has always been true.
"Sights and sounds signifying nothing"
are difficult to understand.
Overwhelmed senses seek sanctuary.
Dulled ones lead us to a lull in our awareness.
The evolving process of being
is an eternal,
an omnipresent,
presenting opportunities
to adopt a point of view that demands integrity
as the pedestal upon which we stand
wobbles in the wind.

LEST WE FORGET

Lest we forget …
In the urban crevasses
and at the edges of the urban jungle
there are beasts of madness.
Yes, we know the vast majority
of humankind is just that
– kind.
They are purposeful.
They plan to live.
Yet others plan to kill and die.
In this new wilderness of our time,
the ever-increasing urban interface,
we must be ever vigilant
as we walk among our own.

THE OLD RANGER

There was,
along trails of my beginnings,
a man, a father,
a Forest Ranger,
a fellow human being.
He was one of those "surrounding" circumstances
that accompanies us all.
I can't remember a "first thought" of him.
It must be that he was always there.
And yet,
I must rely on others for that confirmation.
So, I trusted someone.
Trust must have its roots in relationships of time.
The more time, ostensibly, the more trust.
It is only in later moments
that we parse and reflect to see if information
fits our "it must be true" template.
I have owned him as my own.
It's sad that parents become so common,
we just take them for granted –
until we lose them.
I remember seeing him working in the woods
for the first time.
He stood like a giant upright bear
stripping bark from a bolt.*
Then,
as I watched in amazement,
he knelt beside a "great tree."
Silently, gently, moving back and forth,
the "Swede" saw's teeth making hardly a sound,
he felled the giant tree.

*A short (5-foot) log.

A momentous occasion,
the loud swishing and thunderous cracking
as the branches
scraped, cracked, and broke,
even driving some into the ground.
Were there "mundane" moments?
Certainly!
And yet …
there was so much more,
as there always is
with retrospection and with age.
To each season of my memories
there were incandescent flashes.
Some were caught
in awe and the appreciation
of a child's mind.
Others, distilled in the winery of time,
were the gifts of experience.
Whether instantaneous
or hard-scrabble wisdom,
they have all come to form a world-view.
The context of these "findings"
have their own allure,
and so it is that I begin.

* * *

First memories'
stickiness know their own purpose.
They are what they are
because they are.
It is only when we begin
the artful practice of recollection,
engage that inner dialog of being,
that our world-view becomes our own.

When,
in the shadows of my mind,
I realized he and He would always be there –
that consequences followed missteps,
did I relate an importance
to an if/then logic connecting means to ends.
For the most part
these were temporal futures
running on the film of my mind.
It took some time
to sort out the difference
between this world and the next.
Perhaps because I was immersed
in the omnipresence of the natural world.
The "woods" was always there
with its muted light
and horizons of the unknown
lost in the dense beyond.
There was always an attention
that needed to be paid to make the next step.
A constant lifting of the eyes
from forest floor to the immediate surrounds
accompanied our every move.
Each trail of adventure,
interspersed with brief pauses,
offered tidbits of information to a curious mind.
Tree identification from leaves
scattered on some unknown path,
tracks of a forest creature,
signs of previous human presence,
all treasures "left to tell"
of other beings' passings,
were always duly noted.
Seldom did we follow laid-out trails.

Pathways always seemed guided
by some silent other presence.
It wasn't until much later
that I realized what dictated the paths taken.
Eventually I came to know
it was a complete and overwhelming confidence
that came from a feeling
– the forest was ours.
We were the supreme architects
of our own freedom.
When we were there,
there was no other place
that we could otherwise be.
A marvelously pure focused form
of a very personal existentialism
was born of those mostly silent moments.
An unleashing of a deep and profound
imagination was allowed to flourish.
And the beauty of this
was that there would be myriad opportunities
to "check"
the potential of one's fathoming
whether they were of him –
arresting violators,
quenching forest fires, cruising timber,
or logging.
Or they were of me.
Could I "fly" from log to log,
from rock to rock?
Could I run flat-out
through the forest's leavings
and still retain my balance?
Were imaginings from infinite intonements
to be rewarded by my sightings?

What games could be played!
And so it was …
I became a bit of a trickster,
a player, a singer, a dancer
under Nature's canopy.
The variegated deciduous,
the flat/round of the evergreens,
the lyrical and the stark,
they all sheltered me
from The Great Beyond.*
In the forest of my time,
I was born free.
Later, I was to learn,
from my early socializations,
the human person
was not so easy to comprehend.
Subjects of the school curriculum
interested me,
but the forest enthralled me.
It wasn't until I went to college
and was exposed to the ideas of the ages
that my mind began to enjoy the forests of the heart,
the craigs and depths of the emotional,
the spiritual trials,
and the inspiration of the physical
in the human realm.
There were classes taken and taught,
semesters, quarters, summers,
and years full of them.
Degrees and still more degrees faded into time.
And yet …
In the course of it all,
I continued to wonder about beginnings and endings.

* "The Great Beyond," from *The Twelfth Hour: A Collection.*

Where were other stepping-stones,
trails, highways and byways,
that led to the understanding of our presence?
Yes, volumes have been written,
and centuries following centuries are full of tracks
of the being called human.
What sifting and winnowing
provides that sure footing sought by all?
In my searchings,
how often had I thought,
"That's it!"
only to find that
in the brilliant and suffused light of day,
the confusing duskings
and the darkness of the night,
the menagerie,
the plethora of history's efforts
are manifold.
Many years later,
in those reminiscings of age,
I hearkened back to those pathways
and those hidden trails of my father
and wondered –
when did I pick up those fixed stars
that have guided my journey?
Could I illuminate a path for others?
Was there another purpose in these memories?
Undoubtedly!
From the invisible trails to "the island"
in Spring-Run Creek,
to the fire-lanes,
from Devil's Lake Road
to the Potawatami Trail,
from Dead End Road
to the Old Horse Barn,

from Oak Tree Corner
to the McAlpine Grade,
from Spy Glass Hill
to Pondevron,
from the Old Liethen Road
to the Pine Plantation,
from the myriad Hidden Pockets
of Timber Ranch
there were provided
the many moments of
"in-between,"*
a storybook of treasures,
wisdom shed from the Old Ranger.

I   Be one! Taken to mean: Be yourself.

II   Stand still in silence! Listen to the depths of the present.

III   Sort out true, not true, and yours, not yours, from the machinations of the world.

IV   Own the truth right now! When you know it, really know it, you had better be busy owning it and sharing it.

V   Act in love! Love is the only all-important activity.

VI   Dedicate yourself to growth! Only in becoming more of what is already there can we be saved from ourselves for ourselves and for others.

VII   The Holy is at hand! Recognize it. Become a part of it. Share the magnificence of the All.

---

* "In-Between Time," from *Always Extolling: A Collection.*

These are "pieces"
from the Old Ranger.
Gifts sifted from his silence
and his terse commentary as it broke
the pace on the pathways of my yesterdays.
How long it took me to sift the chaff of my paths
to the wheat of his harvests!
Years of more-thans and less-thans
had blinded and placed stumbling blocks
in paths laden with too much of this
and not enough of that.
"Be responsible for what you know,
and pray that you do not forget your God."
Thanks! Old Ranger.